T0156834

You're Only As Sick As Your Secrets

Sexual Abuse Awareness, Prevention and Intervention

Donna Jacques Temm

BALBOA.
PRESS

Balboa Press books may be ordered through booksellers or by contacting:

Balboa Press
A Division of Hay House
1663 Liberty Drive
Bloomington, IN 47403
www.balboapress.com
1-(877) 407-4847

Because of the dynamic nature of the Internet, any Web addresses or links contained in this book may have changed since publication and may no longer be valid. The views expressed in this work are solely those of the author and do not necessarily reflect the views of the publisher, and the publisher hereby disclaims any responsibility for them.

The author of this book does not dispense medical advice or prescribe the use of any technique as a form of treatment for physical, emotional, or medical problems without the advice of a physician, either directly or indirectly. The intent of the author is only to offer information of a general nature to help you in your quest for emotional and spiritual well-being. In the event you use any of the information in this book for yourself, which is your constitutional right, the author and the publisher assume no responsibility for your actions.

ISBN: 978-1-4525-0027-0 (sc)
ISBN: 978-1-4525-0030-0 (e)

Library of Congress Control Number: 2010935775

Printed in the United States of America

Balboa Press rev. date: 10/8/2010

Dedicated to Mom and Dad with more love than written words could ever express. I love you both!

For my son, Dylan, who is my reason...
I thank God for you every day and love you with all my heart.

And my brother, Gary, who has been my spiritual source of inspiration and guidance throughout this whole process.

1959 - 1995

Many, many, many special thanks to all who have crossed my path. Too numerous to mention and one not more important than another in my journey of healing. I will forever hold you in my heart with a sense of gratitude and appreciation.

Dear Reader,

Intention...

My intentions for writing this book are numerous. Initially, it was primarily about knowledge. I had the intention of reaching all who would be willing to pick up this book, whether a parent or guardian, professional advocate or therapist, teacher or child care provider, medical professional or other caregiver of any type. I intended to share whatever I could to allow for recognition of something that could so easily be masked and overlooked unintentionally.

As the words spilled onto the pages, I then had the hopeful intention that this little book would fall into the hands of those beautiful individuals who so needlessly endured (and quite possibly continue to do so) the horrific, devastating, life-altering actions of any type of abuse.

Throughout the process of writing my story with the intention of bringing healing to others, I began to realize that I, too, was being healed through reading my written words as they formed a cohesive story of my life thus far. I believe that, in itself, to be the intention of an all-loving, all-knowing source that is greater than myself. Call it the universe. Call it God. Call it a combination.

I am filled with gratitude and am thankful for the many blessings in my intention to pay forward the sincere kindness and compassion showered upon me by the many, many magnificent souls who have so positively impacted my journey.

Finally, it is my intention that love and light surround you and infuse each and every one of your actions.

Respectfully,
Donna Temm

CONTENTS

Through the Eyes of the Inner Child

I was the youngest of many nieces
Yet, it was my life he tried to shatter to pieces.
I'd made him angry that Christmas night
I'd had it coming 'cause I wasn't nice.
What happened later, this four year old could not comprehend
I only knew I could not tell even my closest friend
And so it went day after day
I worked hard not to give that secret away.
Going to bed became my biggest fear
I'd lay awake all night so I'd see and hear.
Each and every morning, I'd wake up feeling sick
"She's just nervous about school – just another trick."
Out the door I'd go with a pasted smile
With dread in my body all the while.
It's amazing how your mind knows to protect and defend
It throws you into a whimsical world of pretend.
And so for the next twenty-eight years
The memories faded but left my fears.
Dis-ease crept into every moment of all my days
Eventually it became known as just another phase.
I became this person I'd never known
Who I really was could never be shown.
Of my thoughts and actions I felt such shame
It was always on others I'd placed the blame.
And try as I might not to cause any commotions
It was taking a toll on all my emotions.
Eventually it led to many types of illness
When ironically I strove for physical wellness.
Soon everyday routines became overwhelming tasks
It was then I began having panic attacks.
It was evident to me I was going crazy
To others it maybe looked as though I was lazy.
Even being in my home made me so tense
What was happening just didn't make sense.

I scolded myself to deal with my fear
But try as I might, symptoms would reappear.
I began living my life in a sort of "protective bubble"
Before I realized it, my marriage was in trouble.
I know now help was sent from God up above
Through prompting of an earth angel, my sister, I love.

So began my counseling with which I'm not through
Yet, I'm learning to show my true self to you.
Through EMDR, I was able to remember
The dreadful details of that initial act in December.
I learned at 33 my actions were not the cause
He was a man with a problem and many flaws
I'm happy to say I don't have to please everyone
I'm now certain I wasn't the cause of what he had done.
Although this journey is a difficult one
I am strong and will survive when all is said and done.
So if you're feeling at your wit's end and parts of this story sound familiar My Friend
Please don't hesitate or think twice; get yourself some caring expert advice.
No matter how untrue you may think it seems
We all have the potential to live up to our dreams!

Chapter 1

Illusions ~
The Ultimate Denial

"Oh my God! I'm so lucky! I can't even imagine!" This was the chatter running through my mind as I sat at the grouping of uneven desks. I looked at my colleagues dispersed around this same set of desks each sitting somewhat uncomfortably. I tried to decipher if the discomfort arose from the small chairs made to perfectly fit lower elementary students or if it was from the agenda of that morning's meeting.

In a week or so, our 1st through 3rd grade elementary school would be hosting a play about sexual abuse. The woman sitting with us was explaining this play's powerful message and informing us of the correct procedure should any of our students disclose information about such a situation. The school district had even gone as far as to provide an additional guidance counselor at the school that morning to ensure each child in crisis would receive immediate support.

Before ending the meeting, this same woman directed her attention to each and every one of the eight teachers in attendance. She went on to tell us the high percentage of adults who had been sexually abused as a child. She encouraged us to seek professional help if any memories were to surface for any one of us.

My mind immediately shot back to my carefree childhood days; a mom and dad not separated by divorce; family vacations with relatives (not really related but close enough to call "aunt" and "uncle"); summers spent at our beach house swimming by day and playing kick the can with siblings and neighborhood children by night; happy holidays with my two aunts playing Hawaiian guitars and the rest of us joining in the singing of French songs. Boy, those were the days! Yes, I had my fears and fair share of "down times", but dealing with students in crisis put my own childhood woes into perspective.

The meeting ended with the ringing of the bell and as was the norm, this day began with those energetic little ones filling the halls. Most were bundled with their winter gear; boots, hats, mittens, snow pants and scarves, not to mention backpacks and lunch boxes. But as could be predicted, not all our little ones would be so bundled. (Some were intentional episodes of leaving behind the winter layers and others were just signs of their harsh realities.)

As I made my way down the hall, the guidance counselor informed me we would need to "chat" before the play took place. I nodded in acceptance and without another moment's hesitation, began yet another day of what I'd been doing for nearly 11 years; pouring my heart and soul, intellect and emotion, into my work to provide nothing but my best for my students.

The day of our little "chat" arrived and the only item on the agenda was a student in my class. She was a second grader, just seven years old. We were all concerned about her welfare and had suspicions about sexual abuse. She was self-mutilating on a daily basis, and her mom (and therefore, she and her siblings) was living with a known sex offender. Nothing could be done. All hands were tied UNLESS this hurting child would disclose to us. This would provide a basis for investigation. Hence, the reason for this meeting. I was encouraged to be open and aware of any opportunities that may arise when she would feel comfortable enough to reach out and trust that she'd be supported. Although a huge responsibility initially, her case would then be handled by authorities and professionals trained in this line of intervention work. I took this task very seriously since I believed that for 181 days these students were mine. I felt the need to care for them on all levels; their education and emotional well-being as well as their physical well-being.

On the day of the play, the whole school arrived downstairs in our basement/cafeteria/gymnasium/auditorium; in other words, our multi-purpose room. The stage was set and the play began. Throughout the presentation, I found myself on edge. Periodically, I needed to remind myself to breathe, release my fisted hands, and drop my shoulders. I attributed it to the fact that my eyes were watching not only my little one in crisis, but also the reactions of all those around her. I wouldn't want to miss an opportunity to help a child, especially one in crisis.

Once the play was finished, I ushered my students back to the classroom and had them all sit on the rug so we could talk about what we'd just witnessed. After one student related his feelings and a personal experience similar to the one in the play, several others began to feel more comfortable and tell of their own experiences. I was appalled at just which children were disclosing. These were children who appeared to have families that didn't "fit" the category of exposing themselves to situations that would allow such instances to occur. At the same time, I was relieved that they had disclosed to their parents and the end results were positive.

It was not until we ended our discussion and headed back to our desks that my little one in crisis oh-so-quietly approached me asking to see the guidance counselor. I immediately got coverage for my class and brought her myself.

Later in the day, I was informed that we had, in fact, received a disclosure and the appropriate phone calls and notifications had been made. The process had begun and I was reassured my little one would be in good hands.

The day ended. Though I was emotionally and physically exhausted, I had a sense of satisfaction. I had hope that the sun would rise just a little brighter tomorrow for one seven-year-old little girl.

Chapter 2

Reflections In Little Mirrors

As I reflect on my first few years of teaching, I realize I was drawn to two students in particular. Each had separate issues. The fact that these issues stemmed from their home situations was their only common thread. I felt their pain as though it was my own and went above and beyond to "fix" or provide whatever they were lacking. It wasn't until years later that I realized these children were mirroring to me and outwardly expressing through their words and actions my own inner repressed painful experiences. Though I was not consciously aware of it, my subconscious mind as well as the memories stored there and throughout my body were being triggered. I was reliving my own past through their ever-present circumstances. I was trying to provide for them what I knew from experience they needed on a core level; a goal I could never accomplish. What they needed did not lie within me, but from somewhere I had no control over.

People who understood this more than I did (counselors and other veteran teachers) had told me that it was in my best interest to emotionally detach from these students. In other words, I was to remember that it was my job to provide each with the best educational experience as well as a safe environment where they could feel confident enough to take educational risks. Beyond that, I could not "fix" their home lives nor could I "fix" their emotional and physical pain whose root causes were beyond my ability to access. The most I could do was to be aware of and recognize any signs of abuse and/or neglect and report it to those professionally trained in such areas of intervention.

I finally came to the realization that I was limited in my options and that detaching from them emotionally was something I could not do. Therefore, I needed to physically detach from them. So when I began to become dissatisfied with other areas of the teaching profession, I finally made the break. Though physically detaching did not erase from my mind what I knew all too well about the circumstances of many children in society, not being subjected to it on a daily basis provided me with a temporary bandage; a bandage that would allow me to look deeper into my own inner turmoil and do the necessary healing.

As I continue on my journey (and it is a continuous journey), I often reflect on my own growth and the opportunities that have presented themselves in my life now. I realize that it has come full circle. My personal experiences with abuse and neglect as well as the healing experiences that stemmed from them are now being shared with so many others in a variety of ways; be it volunteering to work with battered and abused women or welcoming more children in similar circumstances into my current profession. Here I have an opportunity to share my story as well as my own triumphs. I can attempt to provide them with some sense of hope through suggestions about approaches and alternatives that allowed me to heal.

I would encourage anyone experiencing great difficulty with the behaviors or life patterns of those around them to look more deeply into their own lives. There is a set of Universal Laws that includes the Law of Reflection (in metaphysical, not scientific terms). Though I won't go into great detail about it, I believe it to be worthy of mention. It states that when there is judgment about something, it can lead to understanding about who we are as well as what we have had as a part of our life experiences. This was evident in the strength with which I felt my students' pain around the area of abuse. Though still on a subconscious level, I was looking into their little faces and they were mirroring my own similar experiences.

Through this book, it is my hope to reach beyond the physical and/or educational training borders within which I've been restricted thus far. It is my intention to bring awareness to a whole different sector of people with direct access to both children of abuse and neglect as well as adult survivors who may still be unaware of their repressed memories but are suffering from dis-ease with inexplicable causes. My hope is to reach those just coming to consciousness who may not be trusting the information they are feeling, those who may be questioning if such thoughts and feelings are fabrications of their own minds, and those who are beginning to believe that they are "going crazy" or suffering from some mental disorder. Within my words, I hope to bring healing.

Chapter 3

The Journey Begins...

My son was in bed and my husband was sitting in his chair. The TV was on, but I can't tell you what we were watching. I was laying alone on the loveseat in my living room. Though my legs were uncomfortable from hanging over the edge, I didn't have it in me to move. I was exhausted on all levels. Though I looked like the most "together" person to the outside world, my inside world was crumbling. By day, I sported a smile and tried to accomplish everything I did to perfection. In the evening, my family got every last bit of my energy. But lately, my "tank" was running low. A good night's sleep no longer refilled it and I was sure I was running on reserves. My logical mind tried to put it all together, but it just couldn't provide me with any insight.

I tried to reason with myself. I'd been through a lot. My health hadn't been the best for quite some time. My marriage was rocky; though I knew of much worse situations. My son had been very ill for several years and doctors couldn't pinpoint the cause, but somehow, his health was recently improving. It had already been nearly six years since my brother had passed away at age 35. I repeatedly told myself I had a good life and I should be thankful for what I had. This was just the type of self-chastising I always did.

That's when I received a phone call that would alter the path of my future. My sister had called at that crucial moment when despair from the depths of my being was so close to the surface that even a positive inflection of my voice was difficult to muster. Just from the tone of my "hello", she knew that something wasn't right.

My sister knew the pattern I'd struggled with for years. I'd dip into periods of undiagnosed depressive states that would continue until my lack of self-compassion kicked in. Then, the next step of the repetitive cycle brought the harsh self-talk as well as the self-chastising. Shame caused me to swallow these feelings, completely disregard my emotions, and resume my unconscious state of being.

Though unaware of the complete details of the conversation that ensued with my sister, I do remember it ending with a very strong, yet supportive, push to seek some professional help. Promising to get some names of well-respected professionals, she ended the conversation with "I love you". Though emotionally and physically exhausted once again, I now had hope that the sun would rise just a little brighter tomorrow for me.

Chapter 4

A Different Perspective

It was several weeks later before I found myself sitting in the office of a counselor who had come highly recommended. Although I could see no legitimate reason for doing so, she made an outline of my family tree, spending time on correctly placing relatives on the appropriate branches.

Next, she asked me to tell her about my past relationships with members of the opposite sex. Because of long courtships, there were very few, yet she wanted to know about each one in great detail. I obliged, though once again unable to understand where she was going with it. After ending with my current relationship, my marriage, I waited in anticipation of what she'd want to hear about next. Much to my surprise, instead of questioning me further, she now had something to add to this one-sided conversation. I was shocked and taken aback when in a very matter-of-fact tone she said, "So you're telling me you've never had a functional intimate relationship with a member of the opposite sex. They've all been dysfunctional." What further shocked me was that there was no tone in her voice conveying a question. She had stated what she believed to be fact.

Confusion quickly turned to disgust. I thought, "Where the hell did she come up with that? That's not at all what I just described!"

But the peacemaker in me chose not to respond in disagreement. The session ended with the scheduling of another appointment for the following week. She handed me a brochure on a process called EMDR. This brochure would provide preliminary information outlining the technique to be used in our next session. Little did I know at that time just how integral it would be in setting the stage not only for a replay of the past but also as an alteration of my future.

The following week's therapy session proved to be extremely different from that of the previous week. I knew from the literature that the EMDR process would focus on unexpressed trauma being stored in the body. I was aware that often such experiences were processed in the emotional brain but never logically reasoned through by the intellectual brain. This is especially common in children. Events perceived as traumatic are stored in a child's body if the brain has not yet formed the synapses that allow communication between the left and right hemispheres. Eventually, unremediated trauma will manifest itself in a variety of ways; often as an emotional imbalance or physical dis-ease.

That day's session entailed focusing on a recalled memory and experiencing it as scenery being viewed from a train's window or from the perspective of watching it on a movie screen. One of two small paddles was placed in each of my hands and alternating vibrations were emanating from each one. A headset displaying alternating beeping tones was also placed on my ears. Though I don't recall the specific memory we were focused on that session, I can say in retrospect that it was nothing that I would have ever imagined would have led to the recovery of a sexual abuse incident.

As my counselor guided me through the process, I was barely aware of the intermittent changes in the speed of alternating beeps and vibrations that were encouraging the transference of information from one brain hemisphere to the other. Though we had a sort of dialogue about the details of what I was recalling, nothing really seemed to be piecing together. The session ended and I was disappointed that no groundbreaking discoveries had been made.

However, off I went with another appointment for the following week to do more of the same work.

Chapter 5

The Realization

At 1:30 a.m., I awoke to my son coughing. Although conditioned to be overly cautious from so many health issues we'd dealt with in his early years, this morning had a sense of heaviness to it. I did all I could to ease his coughing and knew the routine. It would be a matter of waiting out the next 20-30 minutes until the cough would subside and he'd be sleeping comfortably again. I made my way back to bed. Though normal for sleep to be just out of reach at times like this, my body was abnormally tense. I felt a sense of urgency that everything be all right immediately. I could feel panic washing over me; yet, my mind could not grasp the logic behind it. In an attempt to either calm me down or to get some sleep himself, my husband offered to go sleep with my son. Normally, I would do so myself, but for some reason, he offered and I accepted. Having to teach the next day and needing at least eight hours of sleep a night, I was already behind the eight ball.

As I lay in bed alone, my mind was racing as quickly as my body was tensing. Sitting up, I turned on the light, grabbed a notebook, and began to journal. Writing whatever popped into my mind, there seemed to be no rhyme or reason to the content being spilled onto the pages. In the very next moment, it was as if a hand other than my own was guiding my pen. Once it was written, my eyes scanned over that dreadfully powerful statement, "I think I've been sexually abused!" Within seconds, it had registered in my brain and doing its job, had sent out a message to the rest of my body.

Being completely consumed by my body's physical reaction and fighting nausea, I quickly closed the notebook and hid it. I made my way downstairs and continued to frantically pace back and forth, back and forth, stopping only to heave.

The rest of the early morning hours were spent sitting on the couch in disbelief trying unsuccessfully to sip tea, then pacing, then heaving, and then repeating the cycle over again. When I came to the realization that this bold statement could, in fact, be true, I began to feel like I was going insane. I had heard of the phrase before and had even said it a few times, but it wasn't until this very moment that I believed I knew what it actually felt like to be on my way to insanity.

By 3:30 a.m., I needed support. This was too big for me to deal with alone and yet I felt the need to keep it to myself or at least from those closest to me. There was such a sense of shame. Two days earlier, after completing my first session of EMDR, my counselor had informed me that it was not uncommon for people to process 24 to 48 hours after such a session. What we didn't discuss was that she had recognized signs (as I would later learn) that pointed to possible sexual abuse. At that time, she gave me her office number as well as her home phone number and told me not to hesitate to call if I felt the need to do so. I graciously accepted thinking that I'd never call her home phone. I believed nothing could be so bad that it couldn't wait until the next scheduled visit.

I found myself going into the basement so as not to wake my family and dialing her office number. After leaving a brief message, I returned to the first floor and began to try to make sense of it all. As I worked my way through possible perpetrators, I shed quiet, frantic tears when I realized that those I loved the most had had ample opportunity to commit such acts. There was a sickening frustration when I wondered about a favorite uncle and yet all I had to go on was a gut feeling that he wasn't "the one".

By 5:30 a.m., I needed to provide some sense of normalcy for myself, so I showered and began to get ready for the day. When my husband awoke, I told him I'd had a rough night and had called my counselor, but that I couldn't talk about it at that time.

Although not my usual self, I made sure to paste that smile on my face by the time my son woke up to begin his day. At 6:30 a.m., the phone rang. Recognizing my counselor's voice, I immediately slipped down to the basement once again where any bit of composure drained from every sense of my being.

I told her of my suspicions of sexual abuse and described the events that had taken place in the hours leading up to this present moment. It was my expectation, or more correctly, my hope, that she would supply me with an explanation about why this was not possible. I waited for her to tell me how it could, in fact, be some sort of fabrication of the mind. However, this was not the case. Instead, she said she needed to see me the first thing that morning. I explained to her that I needed to go to work. When she insisted on seeing me, I went into autopilot. After securing a substitute for my classroom and providing sub plans, I saw my family off on their day and headed to my appointment.

The next seven days still remain a blur. I can tell you I took three days off from work and had three appointments with my counselor. I slept a total of ten hours and ate the equivalent of one, possibly two, meals due to my inability to easily swallow anything, including water. This one thing, however, remained very clear to me; I survived that first week because of the loving, caring support I received from those I allowed to help me.

At that time, my circle of support was a small one due to my difficulty, first with believing, then with speaking of this newly recollected information. Shame, mixed with denial, kept that circle of support very small for a very long time. Initially, it included my sister, my counselor, and my husband. Each assumed very different roles in supporting me. My sister was beneficial in helping me to connect the details into some sense of truth (as you will see in the upcoming chapter). My counselor provided me with support through her knowledge and expertise as well as her assertive manner in which she encouraged me to do what was necessary to get through this time of immediate crisis. As for my husband, his biggest gift of support to me that first week was to respect my inability to share in depth what I was going through. He supported me by allowing me to do whatever was necessary to get me beyond the extremes of what I was currently experiencing.

Within weeks, I would attempt to include one more person into my support system. However, I realized through this person's gift of truth that not all have the ability to be actively involved in being of support to another. What was always very clear to me, though, was the knowledge that ultimately this individual loved me greatly and wanted nothing but healing and wellness for me.

Chapter 6

Support...Finding, Then Allowing

Although she knew I was coming, I'm sure she never expected what she encountered the moment she opened the door. All I'd told my sister when I'd called earlier that day was that I needed to talk to her about something important. We made plans for me to spend the night, an unusual event made even more unusual by the fact I was supposed to work the next day. She lived about 30 extra minutes away from the school at which I taught.

Keeping my composure on the drive there was the easy part. Remaining composed once I arrived would be the challenge. I had been to see my counselor that morning and through another session of EMDR was able to retrieve some of the details of that dreadful event.

I remember my sister opening the door and I immediately began to cry. She embraced me in a hug that would within moments become a physical support. It was as if the dam had broken. As I listened to the wails that emanated from me, I was somewhat frightened. I'd never before heard such sounds from my own mouth. My body began to shake terribly, an experience I couldn't recall having in the past.

After what seemed like an eternity, I was able to pull myself together somewhat and physically support myself again. For the next seven and a half hours, we sat in my sister's living room trying to put the pieces together. Being twelve years older than me, she was able to remember details of circumstances, situations, and physical surroundings that I had been either too young to comprehend or too emotionally repressed to recall.

That morning during my EMDR session, I remembered the incident having taken place in a twin, four-posted bed that was kitty corner in a room. Though I couldn't decipher exactly what room it was in (I would later find out that sometimes several memories will clump together creating confusion when recalling specific details), I was quite certain the placement of the head of the bed was behind a door that swung open toward its left side.

My sister was an immense help to me that night. She remembered the four-posted bed as being a set of bunk beds my parents had detached to make into two separate twin beds for my other sister and me. My bed had, in fact, been placed kitty corner in the room of the house I had come home to as a newborn. This detail, in itself, gave me a time frame as to when the incident had taken place. It had to be before the age of nine since we'd moved into a new house my third grade year. Though she and I worked together to come up with possible perpetrators, it ended in frustration and no further than when we'd begun.

Though proof that the event had actually taken place was starting to come together, I was still in denial. I kept thinking that maybe, just maybe, this was some sort of fabrication on my part and was almost embarrassed that I could very possibly be making a big deal out of something that had never truly taken place. Such thinking can be very common among people who have experienced sexual abuse. For those with resurfacing repressed memories, the loss of the ability to dissociate (split themselves off from their traumas allowing them to function with minimal negative impact) brings about suffering. Now they must feel the pain associated with it. Often this pain, if allowed to stagnate, can lead to depression if remediation techniques are not employed. Such a shattering of one's illusions about life can be devastating.

We decided to try to get some sleep. It was 2:00 a.m. My sister needed to be up for 5:30 a.m. to go to work and I had another session with my counselor that morning. During the night, a petrifying fear had engulfed my whole being and not only was I unable to close my eyes, but I was unable to move my body in any position other than on my back with my face pointed straight toward the ceiling. That way, my peripheral vision could catch any movement around me, and my ears, any sound from any direction.

5:30 arrived, as did my sister, gingerly making her way toward the pull out couch to check on me. I had heard her coming before I had seen her. She found me awake and in the exact same position she'd left me in only hours before. Both exhausted physically from the lack of sleep as well as mentally and emotionally from the previous night's quest for the truth, my sister and I readied ourselves for the day ahead. We shared an embrace before heading off in separate directions; she to work and me to yet another counseling appointment.

Once that initial week of crisis was over, I returned to my "normal life" of working and being a wife and mother. Though I continued to see my counselor once a week for a period of time, the rest remains a blur. To this day, I don't know how I did what I did. My weight dropped dramatically as a typical daily diet for me became a piece of bread and several sips of water. Though I eventually would be able to tolerate the feel of food in my mouth once again, actually swallowing it continued to pose a challenge. I remember seeing people I hadn't seen in quite some time and can vividly recall their reactions of shock. Instead of a congratulatory response to my weight loss, it was more of a jolted recognition.

By Easter of that year, I was still struggling with my eating, especially with the consumption of meats. What had once been my favorite meal of ham and all the "fixins", now became a personal challenge to ingest. With time and a great deal of hard work, I would be successful in overcoming this and many other areas of difficulty.

Chapter 7

The Self-Chastising ~
"Get over it!"

If there was one constant about me, it was my intolerance for people who chose to dwell in self pity and, excuse the expression, sit in their own shit. Now let me clarify what I mean here. I don't judge those who find it difficult to move out of their comfort zones as long as their choices do not impose on others or continue to negatively impact those around them. So it was with this remembrance about who I truly was (and had forgotten to be) that I decided enough was enough. It had been six months and I needed to "get over it"! Though my puzzle was not totally complete and there were crucial missing pieces that remained out of mental reach, I graciously thanked my counselor for all she'd done for me and told her I would no longer be in need of her services.

When I shared with my counselor that in my family when something disappointing takes place, we pull ourselves up by the bootstraps and keep going, she very clearly responded with "Honey, strap yourself in and hang on 'cause you're going for a ride!" That said, I began to rehash what I'd already dealt with on a completely different level.

In our time working together, I had made some great progress. In retrieving the entirety of a crucial memory of one family Christmas party, I was able to put a face and name to the perpetrator. Though the memory set me back dramatically, I had worked hard and courageously to redefine my sense of reality that I'd literally had stripped from me.

As unnecessary as the "depth" of the details of that first memory may be, those details are, in fact, crucial in helping me make a point about the way repressed memories can surface. So it is here that I take you back in time.

* * * * *

As is the norm for many (though not all) children, Christmas was my favorite time of the year. It was always a special holiday in my family, not only for the tradition of the giving and receiving of presents, but also for its significance in the belief of our faith.

As I would be told later, aside from our own intimate, immediate family celebration, we also would celebrate with my dad's family each year. Being the youngest of sixteen children, my dad's immediate family had dwindled in number but had grown with each new addition to their own families. Certain siblings, my dad included, had hosted the family Christmas celebrations on a rotating schedule. The year I was four or five years old, my family hosted the party at our home. We had a great setup for entertaining with an open concept dining and living room, a separate kitchen, and even a ping pong/pool table in the basement. All bedrooms were tucked away on the second floor.

I vividly remember walking from the dining room into the kitchen where my mom was tending to the hors d'ouevres. Aside from a small table in that room, we also had a white wicker rocking chair that happened at that moment to be occupied by a non-blood relative. I can still feel the surprise in my body and the tug on my arm as he reached and grabbed hold of it. I had been on my way to the fun in the basement when he pulled me toward him and wanted a kiss. I wasn't particularly fond of this man and the last thing I wanted to do was give in to his request. Though he pressed the issue for quite some time, he eventually let me go after informing me that he'd get his kiss before the end of the night. Just as soon as he released his grip, I shot off in the other direction and headed for safety with dread in my body. Suddenly, the fun in the basement was no longer enticing and I sat alone and frightened on the darkened stairs leading to the second floor.

As tears rolled down my cheeks, I began to worry about the "end of the night" and how I would get out of giving him a kiss. Just then, this dreadful man's son came up from the basement and happened to notice me sitting on the stairs crying. He took my hand, brought me to the kitchen, and sat me on his lap. In front of his father, he asked me what was wrong. After listening to my predicament, he told me in no uncertain terms that I didn't have to do any such thing. Relief was immediate. The evening ended with going to bed without kissing anyone I chose not to!

This memory was part of my life for years. It was just one of those incidents that remained in my repertoire while others seemed to fade away completely or until something jogged it to return. Eventually, I would learn or at least remember, due to a jogging from yet another session of EMDR, what had truly transpired that Christmas evening.

Chapter 8

A Memory Unfolds

"Just think of it as being on a train where you're watching the scenery go by but yet you are removed from it." This was the advice I received from my counselor as we prepared to do an EMDR session on this particular Christmas memory. We began the session with vibrating paddles in each hand and earphones displaying alternating beeps in my left and right ears. As I began to process the events of that night, I received validation that the long-held memory had, in fact, happened the way I'd previously described it. However, what became evident was that the incident did not end as memory would have it. This dreadful man would find his way to my room later that evening taking much more than the kiss he claimed I owed him...

* * * * *

Because the sister with whom I shared a bedroom was four and a half years older than me, she was allowed to stay up later. I went off to bed that evening while the party was still in full force. As I lay in bed, the room was only dimly lit from the streetlights illuminating the area around the sides of the window shades. Suddenly, the door swung open and in toward the left side of my bed. For a moment, all I could make out was the shadow of a figure entering my room. From the shape, height, and mannerisms, I didn't recognize it as a member of my immediate family checking on me. Within moments, this figure was on top of me and so much in my face that I could distinctly smell the alcohol on his breath. His body was very heavy on mine and I found it difficult to move or even take a breath. I was frightened, as I had no idea of what was transpiring. My inability to comprehend the situation did not deter the fact that my mind and body sensed it to be so very wrong!

The next thing I remembered was our family pet, a beagle, wandering into my room and sitting at the very edge of the right side of my bed. It is my belief that she was the cause of his departure. He was concerned she would bark and bring attention to that room of the house. Moments later, he left the room without even looking back ~ an action of total disregard. However, my dog never left the room, nor did she lie down or move a muscle from the edge of that right side of my bed where she stayed for the night's entirety.

Terrified and shaking beyond belief, I stayed in my room. Once in bed, it was an unspoken rule in our home that you were not to get up unless you were sick or had to use the bathroom. In an innate sort of attempt to self-soothe, I made my way over to my stuffed animals and dolls scattered around my bedroom. Once back in bed, I placed them all around me creating a barrier between myself and anything that might come into contact with me. It was at that moment that I believe I first began dissociating, a defense mechanism or maybe even a survival technique I would later employ regularly in my life.

The dawn not only brought comforting light, but also a source of relief when my mom peeked into my room and found me already awake with my dog still in the exact same spot she'd been in since entering my room the night before. Little did my mom know I hadn't slept at all. After a comment about being up so early, Mom took my hand and together we made our way downstairs.

Chapter 9

The Harsh Reality

One question kept playing over and over in my thoughts.
Why, as a child, hadn't I told someone what had been going
on? Less than a year after I'd decided I needed to "get over
it" and "go it alone" (a pattern I would continue to repeat and still
to this day unconsciously fall back on from time to time), I found
myself sitting in my counselor's office once again. A harsh reality
had slapped me in the face and it stung so badly that it sent me
back more than a few steps. What I thought had been one isolated
incident now made way for additional, multiple incidents and I was
unsure of when the memories would stop surfacing. Up to this point,
all incidents had occurred on the Christmas holidays. This explained
the reason for my panic in recent years every Christmas Eve. On
those occasions, my conscious mind hadn't remembered yet, but
my subconscious mind, as well as my body and its cellular memory,
remembered all too well.

* * * * *

As a child, after the first incident, I became very fearful of my
room and bedtime. I can vividly recall my mom trying to help me
through what appeared to be another "phase". Children go through

phases all the time. As a parent, it is hard to decipher not only what is appropriate developmental behavior but also how much attention to give to each "phase" without making a "mountain out of a molehill". In my opinion, my mom went above and beyond to try to fix something about which she actually had no idea. At that time, I wanted my bed moved and she put it facing the door exactly as I had requested. A new yellow and white comforter and curtains were bought to redecorate my room and to help brighten it. She even made a ceramic clock to match. I was allowed to leave on the lamp on my nightstand next to my bed all night.

For a while, all requests were met and though I went to bed more easily in my parents' eyes, I was still extremely, yet quietly, fearful in that little body of mine. Therefore, I was sleeping very little. My eyes were zoned in on the top of the stairs and my ears were busy listening for anyone who may have been approaching. However, without this knowledge, my parents blamed the lamp for my lack of sleep and within a short period of time, it was no longer allowed to stay on. Because of the panic that ensued in the darkness, the hall light was kept on until my parents went to bed each night. Yet, I continued to have trouble sleeping. Because of my secrecy, they had no other reason but to believe the hall light to be the contributing factor.

Finally, the light in the hall was kept on, but the door was closed a bit, just enough so I could no longer see the stairs and had to rely solely on my sense of hearing. If you've ever been somewhere with closed eyes and focused on what you were hearing, I'm sure you were amazed at how many sounds you noticed to which you probably had never before paid any attention. If you have not done so, I challenge you to do so now. Take a few moments to stay quiet, being sure to keep your eyes closed at all times and listen to the sounds you hear. You'll be shocked at what your ears pick up and how your mind will be highly aware of and/or reactive to these sounds. Now, add fear to the body and watch your imagination run wild.

Soon after the door was kept only slightly ajar, I slipped into my world of make-believe each night. I would play house in my bed for hours, whispering conversations that went on between my stuffed animals and my dolls. This was another way of dissociating. Looking back, I now recognize how this was just one more way my mind took over and allowed me to survive.

My third grade year, we moved into a new house. I made many changes that year, one being my choice to cut my hair. I had always loved long hair and had been growing it out for quite some time. Looking back at my third grade class picture, I had a very different look. Not only was my long hair gone, but so was my smile. For the first time, I looked more like a boy just as I had intended. It was just another one of my plans to possibly have some control over what had been and still was happening to me.

Looking forward into the ensuing years, I now am able to recognize how I continued this pattern periodically. At times, even in my adult life, my clothing style and color choices were a direct indication of my emotional and physical states. Often, dark colors and loose-fitting clothing falsely aided my attempts to "just disappear" or not call attention to myself.

As a child, one constant for me was my continued lack of sleep and my growing hatred for going to bed. So it was then that I decided to take up swearing. Going to a Catholic school, I knew it was wrong, but yet I was desperate. You see, it was my way of connecting with my dad each evening. In later years, my family and I got quite a chuckle looking back on it. We called it my "going to confession" every night.

My dad owned a car dealership. He'd work until 8:00 every evening and would arrive home by 8:20. I'd already be in bed but would hear the garage door opening just below my bedroom. He'd open the door to the closet in the hallway and this is when the routine would begin and progress as follows...

"Dad?"

"Yes."

"Can you come here for a minute, please?"

"I'll be right there." The closet door would close and within three seconds, my bedroom door would open. He would stand near my bed and very patiently ask, "What's the matter?" (like he didn't know from the night before, or the night before that, or even the night before that)

"I said 'shit' today," I'd tell him genuinely and sincerely sad that I'd done so.

"That's O.K., just don't say it again," he'd reply very matter-of-factly before bending down and giving me a kiss. He'd leave the room knowing all too well that within 24 hours, I'd indeed swear again and our little routine would continue.

As an adult, there was much self-questioning about some of my childhood behaviors. One specifically was why I'd never told anyone about what had been happening. I had two parents who loved and protected me. Anytime they went away, they only left me with family members they trusted. They even went as far as to threaten to sever a friendship with someone I'd been allowing to emotionally take advantage of me. So why wouldn't I have told them about the abuse when I'd had so many opportunities to do so?

It wasn't until years later, through counseling, I'd receive my answer. It would come with the memory of a very important detail. This detail would also provide the reason why it was so important for me to go to "confession" every night, specifically to my dad.

Up to this point, I'd only remembered the physical and sexual abuse. But like many perpetrators, this abuser had incorporated emotional, mental, and verbal abuse. In uttering the following words, he ensured my cooperation in secrecy:

"IF YOU TELL ANYONE, I WILL KILL YOUR FATHER!"

Wow, talk about a boatload of responsibility placed on a very young child. I was now responsible for my father's life. I knew I had to hide all "negative" emotions and feelings. If it got to be too much, and I accidentally broke down and began to cry or got so anxiety stricken that I became physically ill, I needed to come up with some excuse as to why I was feeling this way. It was my perception that I could never, ever, ever tell the truth! My dad's life was in the palm of my tiny little hands! If my dad were killed, it would be horrible. To make matters worse, I wondered what would happen to my mom if my dad weren't around? If something happened to my mom, what would happen to my siblings and me? These concerns prompted me to do the daily check-in, or "confession", with my dad so I could see for myself that he was alive and unharmed for yet another day.

Chapter 10

Food For Thought On Awareness, Prevention, and Intervention

The perpetrator had taken so much from me, including my power, and I had allowed him to do so. Being so young, I didn't understand that I had choices. Unfortunately, this is the case with the majority of children. In allowing "children to be children," we want them to keep that innocence for as long as possible. Despite what I've personally been through, I continue to struggle with trying to strike a balance between informing my own son and allowing him to wallow in that childhood innocence for as long as possible.

I'm not saying we should allow our children to walk through life without the tools necessary for awareness and self-care. I believe prevention is the ultimate goal. However, I am also looking at life from a realistic perspective. Societal influences do not allow us to be with our children 24/7/365. The reality is that things happen, both beautiful and horrendous, and we have to be prepared for either. In each lifetime, there will be moments that take our breath away; some by the beauty that surrounds us on a daily basis, and others by the split-second, unfortunate happenings that have the potential to forever alter our lives.

The question remains as to how to provide such education without placing unnecessary fear into them. It's a very difficult issue to discuss with children. I am not an expert in this area and cannot and will not hand out specifics on "what to do and what not to do". Though I don't have the "cure-all" answers for you, I only offer the following as advice in hopes it will help to empower you.

Every child is developmentally, genetically, emotionally, physically, etc. unique. What one can process at a certain age, another may only begin to grasp at another age. So I encourage parents/caregivers to keep the lines of communication open by being aware and asking non-threatening, yet provoking questions and then actively listening. Try to avoid any questions easily answered with a "yes" or "no" response. Engage your child in conversation about a topic they may be desperately trying to avoid. Watch for body language. Look beyond certain behaviors to the root of the issue. Don't just accept things as they are if they just don't "feel" right to you. Educate yourself by seeking expert advice, if necessary, through a counselor or child advocate. Knowledge is never wasted and it is my belief that when a child is in crisis, time is of the essence.

Most important of all (and I cannot emphasize this strongly enough) is the following statement that many of you may, upon first reading, find offensive and maybe even appalling. However, upon reflection, you may come to understand or view it differently. Some will have experienced firsthand what I write while others, still, will not be able to come to accept it at all.

So here it is: It is my opinion based on my own experiences that although such an experience is extremely detrimental, life-altering, fear instilling, power stripping, physically, emotionally, and spiritually damaging (and the list goes on), it is even more so if the injustice is not quickly ascertained and rectified. It (again, in my opinion) is imperative that the abused be immediately supported, protected, removed from further harm, counseled, and whatever else is deemed necessary and of benefit.

A disclosure must always be taken seriously and the seriousness of it should never be diminished. A support system must be built for these individuals with professional assistance as a part of that system.

It is also my belief that with early intervention, the harmful lasting effects can be kept to a minimum. One of the most important things you can do for yourself or someone you know who is being or has been sexually abused (or abused in any way for that matter), is to get the appropriate, necessary help immediately. It's bad enough that the abuse transpired, but to have to deal with the repercussions alone only continues to compound the problem. That is when survival strategies and cognitive coping patterns form which are difficult to sever when no longer needed or appropriate.

For example, as an adult having experienced abuse in my childhood, there are times I am confused by my own behaviors and actions. Often I don't immediately recognize the connection to the abuse as a child. Though I don't want to play the victim nor go to a place of self-pity, it is important for me to look at the role my past has played and continues to play in my life.

For years, even before the repressed memories began to surface, I was obsessed with protecting my child. Everything I did for him or that related to his welfare was such a serious matter in my eyes. Once the reality of my childhood hit, my seriousness as a parent quadrupled as did my ability to understand my behavior. It was also at a time when he was more involved in outside activities. He now had birthday parties he was invited to that Mom was expected to drop him off at and return several hours later to pick him up. His invitations to sleepovers at friends' houses (a natural stage in growing up) would send me over the edge. On the one hand, I wanted him to be normal and have fun as a child; but on the other hand, I'd allow these events to work me into a complete physical and emotional wreck.

Over the years, I've realized just how difficult "anniversaries" can be. When I speak of anniversaries, I mean those times that trigger crucial aspects of certain childhood ages of my own. For example, the repressed memories began surfacing at the time my son turned four and five years old; the age I was when the abuse began.

Years later, I found my anxiety level heightened the summer before my son entered eighth grade. My son's typical thirteen-year-old behaviors began causing immense concern on my part. I found myself having repeated conversations with him asking if everything was all right or if he felt he needed to talk to me about anything. I even went as far as eluding to the fact that if there was something deeper causing his outward behavior it was important he tell me because I could only help him if he let me know what was truly going on.

Though I knew I was making a bigger deal out of something that was probably truly nothing unordinary in a thirteen-year-old's life, I was unable to just let it be. In doing my own emotional work, I was able to understand my urgency with my son. It was the summer before my own eighth grade year that I had begun planning my suicide. The "anniversary" had triggered that repressed memory and until it surfaced, I was on high alert. Understanding this allowed me to stop projecting my own "stuff" onto my son.

Another example of my past having a direct impact on my current behavior is the dread I felt about being the guest of honor at a party celebrating my 40th birthday. I wanted nothing more than to just let the occasion slip by with only little recognition. The people closest to me were the most perplexed by this. I was also unsure as to why this was so. I had no problem, emotionally or physically, with turning 40. Yet, upon closer inspection, I realized that I didn't have a large number of close friends. I had many acquaintances, but because of my isolation or inability (or my choice not to) to open up to very few people over the course of those 40 years, I had led a sort of isolated life even with so many people around me. Most of my relationships were very superficial, not because I didn't care deeply about them, but more because I would only allow them to develop to a certain level. I couldn't allow myself to have close friends. With the secret I'd had to keep for so many years, it just took too much energy and was far too dangerous.

As a child and young teenager, I was keeping the secret to literally save the lives of my family members. I couldn't take the chance that someone might slip and it would get back to them, or worse, back to the perpetrator. There were many definites about my family, the most important being the love, care, and respect we felt and showed for one another. As the old saying goes, "Blood is thicker than water." Our blood was definitely thick! All my life, I'd been my family's self-imposed "protector". When the abuse was taking place, I became their physical protector since their lives were being threatened (as explained earlier). When the repressed memories began to surface, the perpetrator had passed away years before so their physical vulnerability was no longer an issue. However, my concern for their emotional well-being now took center stage. I had made it my continued mission to protect them on all levels in any way necessary. This is just another example of outdated survival strategies and cognitive coping patterns still being employed.

Understanding the tie between my current behavior and my past allows for a sense of self-compassion and an awareness that can lead to growth. It also allows for an opportunity to sever those survival techniques and defense systems no longer necessary, yet habitual, since formed so many years before.

Though I still struggle with related issues at times, I've also come to rely on the very important concept I learned through my own personal journey. As touched upon earlier, it is my belief that the biggest travesty was not that the abuse took place (though it was completely devastating) but that it continued to go on unrecognized and therefore, I had no support to help me through the crises. I needed to grow up very quickly and learn to self-soothe as well as develop survival techniques and strategies all on my own.

I find it very important here to be sure all of you are aware that I am in no way placing blame on any people in my life at that time, be it family members, teachers, friends, neighbors, etc. If you recall, keeping the secret was a choice I made based on the threat to my father's life. I became a very tough nut to crack and displaced and projected my feelings and actions in all directions but the one that led to the truth. Through repression, I even kept the truth from my conscious self for decades. However, with awareness, I could now begin to recognize and change these dysfunctional unnecessary thought and behavioral patterns.

Chapter 11

Unacted Upon
Chances for Change

In time, I'd begun to harbor feelings of animosity (for lack of a better word) toward another relative. I refused to visit and all my actions with regard to her were very dismissive. As time went by, I had a sort of disregard for her, not wishing anything bad upon her, but yet, when unfortunate events arose in her life, my usual manner of empathy failed to kick in.

At one point, she had become ill and was brought to the hospital. My parents had been out of state for the winter at that time and, as I can only imagine, felt a sense of urgency to keep close tabs on her health. In feeling so, they asked my sister and me to visit her if possible. Now, it must be said that I would do anything for my parents, especially when requests are made. It was never my parents' way to ask of our time as adults unless it meant a great deal to them. Regardless, I never visited her. Did I have the time? I would have made the time.

It was puzzling to me. Eventually, my disregard had turned to anger and I couldn't quite put my finger on "why". As time went by, I had a hunch that she'd known about the abuse that had taken place, but how could I possibly make such a serious accusation based on an assumption? Looking back now and knowing what I know, I've found that answer. I was doing another form of disregarding, only this time I was disregarding myself, my "gut feelings", and my intuition.

I remembered it this way…

It was yet another family get-together and all were gathered at the perpetrator's house. As was the norm, the adults were sitting around the combined kitchen/dining room area where I chose to stay close to my mom and dad. The teenagers all tended to sit in the living room, just off the dining area. As I remember it, there were reclining chairs, a couch, TV, and too much darkness for my comfort. Drifting light from the dining room through the arched opening was the living room's only light. Even darker than the living room was a hallway and though I can tell you there were bedrooms and possibly a bathroom located in that area, at this time I have absolutely no recollection of ever being in that section of the house.

Just as you entered the living room, there was a bedroom to the right (his) with an attached bathroom. This bathroom that visitors used was also always a very dark room. Talk about literally and figuratively "living in darkness". One particular evening, I needed to use the bathroom. I recall walking through the doorway to the bedroom and noticing a figure (his) standing in the bathroom doorway looking straight at me. Ironically, there was a light on behind him. Not a bright light, but sort of a dim orange glow. At five years old, I knew of no other choice than to do as I was, at that moment, being told to do. End of memory, UNTIL…

Years later, the memory became more detailed and aided in the process of understanding my confusing feelings toward this female relative mentioned earlier. That particular evening I was not feeling well and needed to use the bathroom. Because it was urgent, I had no choice but to go into the bathroom where the perpetrator had been waiting. Even if it had not been an emergency, I knew from past experiences that I must never disobey him. On one occasion, I chose to do so. The next time he got to me, he physically roughed me up, got in my face, called me a little bitch, and asked, "What are you trying to do...get your fucking father killed?" So that night I entered the bathroom where I would have my first encounter with oral sex.

Though I knew nothing of what would happen, I did know by now that previous experiences with the perpetrator had left me frightened, confused, sick, and physically pained. At that time, I didn't know what to do. So I dissociated and went into pretend mode. I began thinking about playing house with my stuffed animals and dolls. I had totally removed myself from the situation except physically.

What had transpired that night was frightening. I was horrified with that all-too-familiar feeling of confusion. I felt as though I was going to be physically sick; yet, somehow, I knew I must regain my composure. And that is just what I did.

When my confused, sickened, frightened little body, mind and soul emerged from that bathroom, it encountered one adult who could have turned everything around for me. She had heard everything that had taken place in that bathroom that night. The look on her face said it all as I'm sure did the look on mine. She could've said something to me...she could've said something to someone, anyone! She could have put a stop to it. She could have saved me from what would continue for nine more long years, all the while, shaping and molding the person I would become and the way I would view the world and approach events in my life. But she didn't. So once again, my life path was altered based on an unacted upon chance for positive change.

* * * * *

When the initial memories surfaced, the perpetrator had already passed away leaving me unable to confront him. Looking back, I believe that was the best way for me. The fear that was riveting through my body upon remembering was so intense. I believe it only would have been intensified had he still been around. However, with this realization, I now had to make a decision of whether or not to confront this female relative. By now, she was elderly and suffering from Alzheimer's Disease. I had visited her years before her mental health began to decline and I recall this one particularly brief (as in getting "cut off" brief) conversation I'd initiated and she'd abruptly and sternly ended.

The exchange began with my comment inferring how difficult it must have been for the perpetrator's son to grow up with the father to which he'd been born. I continued with sharing my understanding of the dysfunction that now plagued this individual. Much to my surprise, her whole demeanor changed and she quickly and angrily informed me that any problems this man had were of his own doing! END of discussion!

Years later, once again, I allowed myself to consider what good could possibly come from another confrontation with this female relative. Would it aid in my healing process? Was her mental health too far gone? Would I have been well-received or would she have just as quickly and coldly shut me off again? And I wondered what my reaction would have been if she were to respond to me in much the same manner as in the past. I was, at that time, a very different person than at the time of the first confrontation.

Next, I continued to question the necessity of another confrontation. Hadn't I already received what I needed simply through remembering? After all, it helped me to gain an understanding of so many of my actions and emotions that make me who I am today. I now understand my anger toward people who completely disregard my thoughts and feelings. It sheds a great deal of light on the teacher that I was and the lengths I would go in order to get my students who were in crisis the emotional and physical support and protection they needed and deserved. The root of my anger and inability to tolerate injustice, especially in situations where children are involved, became quite clear also. The list goes on and on, but the answer was not an easy one.

In the end, her mental capacity in conjunction with my own personal growth aided my decision not to confront her. It encouraged me to allow myself to move beyond this struggle, thereby, continuing on my journey toward overall healing.

Chapter 12

Why Hadn't I Disclosed?

With each memory that surfaced, it felt as though I was catapulted back into a state of fear. It was discouraging to feel as though one memory could so quickly erase all I had worked so hard to gain; self-confidence, overcoming fear, moving beyond my comfort zone and the courage it had taken. Often, I so desperately wanted to fall back into my old survival strategies and at times, that is, in fact, what I did. But being the person I am and having the desperate desire to heal and move forward in my life toward one of thriving versus one of surviving, my stay in my old ways became shorter and shorter with each episode. I was growing stronger and this was evidence of that fact.

As mentioned earlier, there was much turmoil in my adult mind as to why I didn't tell anyone about the abuse. With time and more resurfacing memories, the answer became clear. So often the perpetrator manipulated me by physically and verbally threatening me. I recall one instance when he cornered me and got in my face. He called me a "little bitch" and a "fucking slut". Though when I was young I was extremely frightened by him, I didn't understand the names he called me. However, as I got older and began to understand exactly what these names meant, my feelings went from confusing to shameful.

He would manipulate me and keep me in line by saying, "You'll never know where I'll be. You might walk into a dark room and I'll be behind the door when you shut it. I'll be behind the shower curtain and you won't know I'm there until it's too late!" One thing I was able to comprehend at a very young age was the fear he created around the holiday of Halloween. He told me that someone would rape me and I wouldn't know who it was because of the costume. He also told me, "They can even come in and kill your whole family. Hell, I could even do it and no one would know it was me!" He'd laugh and warn me, "Be careful when you open that door for trick-or-treaters!"

During the acts of sexual abuse, he'd use physical force and restrict my airway just enough to allow breath to flow through but so that no sound could emanate from me. He'd say, "You like this, bitch. You wanted it so you asked for it. You're a bad girl and you're going to hell. I'll see you there. You'll NEVER get away from me!" He'd even tell me that my family didn't love me because they thought I was a pain in the ass and he was just doing them a favor. Though I knew my family did love me, the fact that I also knew I was the "pain in the ass little sister" made me question if what he said was true. That's how he'd play the game; he'd infuse some truth in with the lies to bring about doubt and confusion.

Despite all his verbal brainwashing, I realized that there were several times when I was broken and just desperate enough to take that chance and trust that an adult would be able to find the protection for my father's life had the perpetrator become aware of my potential disclosure. (As memories continued to surface, I realized that there were to my knowledge up to this time in my life at least three times when I tried to reveal the secret I kept so deep inside, away not only from my family and friends, but also from myself.)

The first time I tried to disclose, I was six years old. The abuse had been going on for about two years. I remember sitting in the kitchen one morning feeling so sick to my stomach (as was the norm) and feeling like it was time to tell. My family members were scurrying about accomplishing their normal morning routines. For whatever reason, each in their own time stopped to ask me what was wrong. Knowing so much was at stake, I was wrestling in my young mind not only about what to say, but how to say it. Before I could get the courage up, each lost patience and continued on their way.

The second time I had the opportunity to disclose was when my parents were away for a short time and I was staying with the female relative who had witnessed the abuse and said nothing. One afternoon, we were going to the perpetrator's house to cook him dinner since his wife had passed and he was now alone. One of his sons and his son's wife would be there also so there would be five of us.

I remember the dread in my body as I tried not to show it. Standing at the sink peeling potatoes was nauseating because my back was to him and I was standing in a room full of people I did not trust! When we all sat to eat dinner, my eyes met his and there was nonverbal communication that told me he knew I was thinking this could very well be the moment of reckoning. My immediate family members weren't there needing protection so I could say and do whatever I pleased without fearing for their lives. However, just as he sensed my willingness to take a chance and put it all out there, I also sensed his nonverbal communication and, though silent, it was as threatening to me as any other he physically, verbally, and sexually had sent my way in the past. I remained silent…

A final time I remember trying to disclose was when I was an adult visiting the female relative (as I wrote about earlier). I do now, however, understand the motivation behind her actions that day. You see, if I disclosed to anyone, her secret would also be revealed about how she had said nothing that day she witnessed the abuse that had taken place in the bathroom so many years before. She, too, was carrying a secret of her own.

Now, being in a healthier state with a great deal of healing work in my repertoire, I can do as I encouraged you to do earlier with your own child. I have looked beyond her behavior of not revealing what she'd witnessed that evening in the bathroom to the root cause of her behavior. Knowing the little I do about her own childhood, I can now understand and accept (to some degree) her completely inappropriate, detrimental choice that evening.

Chapter 13

Avenues To Healing

Repressed memories can surface in a number of different ways. It may be through the realization of a memory that didn't end the way you thought it had. It may be through a dream that was particularly disturbing and left you with a nagging feeling throughout the day (although, I caution you to analyze the dream because often a literal interpretation of our disturbing dreams can reveal something very different from a symbolic interpretation). Still yet, a repressed memory may surface in a journal entry.

Many of my repressed memories surfaced during or after some form of bodywork. Although my memories started to surface years before, many more did so after I began schooling for massage therapy. Intense bodywork was being done on me and as I would come to realize, such bodywork can trigger the processing of stored emotions.

Whether a traumatic event has taken place during childhood or well into your adult years, if the body and/or mind cannot comprehend what has transpired or it does not know what to do with it, this event will be stored as a memory someplace in the physical body. This is especially true when the traumatic event has occurred during the early stages of childhood. Often, at this time, the synapses that allow communication between the left and right brain hemispheres are not yet fully formed.

Any traumatic event processed on the emotional side of the brain but unable to be reasoned through on the logical side (due to the lack of formation of these synapses) may be stored in some area of the body. This allows for the potential of the memory to manifest as a dis-ease later in life if some form of remediation or therapy is not employed.

I remember one of my first counselors commenting on how amazed she was that I had not developed some form of a life-threatening disease. That was eye opening for me and it propelled me to learn more about the mind/body connection. The result of this research led me in a whole new direction of therapy when at one point I found myself dipping into that tunnel of depression once again. However, because I had a repertoire of self-care techniques as well as an awareness of when to reach out to others for help, the dips didn't dip quite as low and the rough portions of the ride didn't seem to last as long.

At that point, I went back into counseling with a therapist who provided a very different type of therapy. I had several private sessions with her and she encouraged me to go on an experiential weekend with the originator of PBSP (Pesso-Boydon System of Psychomotor), Al Pesso. His type of therapy included a mind/body connection component.

The weekend was incredibly intense and at some points overwhelming. After each day, I found myself at the inn at which I was staying thinking, "What am I doing here? I don't belong here! What have I gotten myself into?" To make matters worse, in the middle of the first night away, I had another body remembrance. In laymen's terms, this is when the body begins to experience the trauma of the past as if it were taking place at that actual moment. It can be quite a scary thing when you don't know what's happening and when you don't have the tools to work through it. Luckily, that was not the first time I'd experienced such episodes so I was able to ride it out. (In the past, several body remembrance episodes sent me to the emergency room where I left with no explanation of what had transpired and a huge bill.) The end result of that weekend left me with an understanding of what I'd been doing to protect everyone in my family for so many years. With hope, I continued my journey with the next phase of my healing.

* * * * *

Though I am going to give you some background information about PBSP, I highly encourage you to visit Al Pesso's website. The information provided at this site is invaluable not only for those who have in some way been affected by some form of abuse, but also for other traumas which take place in life.

In Webster's Dictionary, a "psychological trauma" is defined as an emotional shock that creates substantial and lasting damage to the psychological development of the individual, gen. leading to neurosis. It is also defined as something that severely jars the mind or emotions. With this information, I ask you, in all seriousness, "Is there anyone walking this earth who has not experienced or been affected by some form of trauma?"

I learned through psychomotor therapy that everyone has six basic needs. The first need is that of belonging/place. Just as stated, we all need a place or home where we feel as though we belong. The second basic need is nurturance; having sufficient food, shelter, clothing, medical care, love, nurturing, and positive touch. The third need is support. This entails having adult help, guidance, and encouragement. Help with problem solving and encouragement to take appropriate risks is a healthy basic need. The fourth basic need is protection or having a safe environment. Limits and emotional containment is the fifth basic need. We all must have appropriate emotional and physical limits set as well as being given permission to express our emotions safely. The final basic need is the need for respect. This entails being valued as a separate person/soul from the parent with appropriate role relationships.

Having a deficiency in one or more areas of some of these basic needs may not seem to constitute a "traumatic" event. However, it is a well researched and therefore, a well known and accepted fact that we all must have our basic needs met at the right time by the right people in the right way. If this does not happen, then there is an area of deficit.

Our experiences mold us into who we become and what we believe about ourselves and the world we live in. So taking it a step further, if we are having difficulty resolving an issue in the "here and now", there is a very good possibility that something that took place in the "there and then" is causing our dis-ease. Psychomotor allows an individual to go back and look at what did not serve us well in the past in hopes of gaining insight into what would have been the most beneficial scenario. It allows us to make a new map, so to speak, through which we can gain a new direction in the present moment.

Some who are unfamiliar with psychomotor may feel that bringing up the past and those who did not provide for our basic needs will only cause hard feelings and additional discontent. However, my experience has been the opposite. When taking a closer look at what actually happened and why, an individual begins to gain a sense of compassion and empathy (on a healthy level) for those people. Often those who were supposed to be providing the basic needs for us did not have their own basic needs met in the "there and then". They were doing the best they could with what they had to work with. Does that excuse their behaviors and make everything OK? Absolutely not! But what it does do is help us to have insight. I've found that my own understanding of my history has helped me to gain a little compassion for myself when I've questioned the quality of my own parenting skills and my effectiveness in providing these basic needs at the right developmental stage for my son.

Chapter 14

A Support System

Despite all the counseling I'd had and the tools I'd been given and had put into practice, at one point in my life, it all became too much for me. Memories were surfacing one after another and there were very few people I could tell them to (or so I believed). I was not only holding onto the information, but I was trying to actually, literally hold myself together. Aside from my counselor, I had a very supportive colleague, but I'd put boundaries around that also. I had wanted to keep clear boundaries between my personal dilemmas and my work setting. In essence, I didn't allow myself to have a very key ingredient in the process of healing; support. There were several other people I occasionally allowed to see me during my worst moments, but despite their best intentions, they often didn't know what to do. Regardless, I was extremely grateful to have them with me and their willingness to do anything within their abilities to help will be forever appreciated.

This one particular day, I had a scheduled visit with my counselor. I walked in feeling numb. Things were not good, but they were not that bad. There were issues that were bothering me, but I didn't see myself as having any control over them so I was resigned to just let them go. The session began and before I was even aware, I was crying on the little antique couch I'd been sitting on. With each moment, my tears began to flow with much more intensity and it seemed like all energy I had to hold and keep myself together vanished.

My counselor wrapped a blanket around me to give me some sense of composure, but to no avail. I just continued to fall apart. To this day, I don't know where I was storing that amount of grief in my body, but it was certainly making its way up and out. On one level, such a release can be cleansing and healing, but my counselor was educated enough to know that, if not channeled in the most efficient way with specific parameters around it, the expression of such strong emotion could actually cause more detriment to me. It was necessary to change those circumstances so that it did not feel as though I was reliving and recreating a similar circumstance of aloneness, despair, and hopelessness (to mention just a few) that I'd experienced at an earlier time in my life.

Finally, she informed me that what she was about to do was not "policy" and asked for my permission to just hold me. With my agreement, she sat beside me and held me while I wept. This provided me with exactly what I'd needed so many times before but had never received due to circumstances both within and beyond my control so many years ago. Within moments, the comfort she gave to me provided exactly what I needed to pick myself up once again and move forward. To this day, I greatly appreciate that incredibly courageous, kind, "out of the box" decision my counselor made at that moment for me that day. It was key since it was my first step in allowing myself to begin to receive from others.

From that experience, I began to trust that if I did reach out, I'd be supported. Little by little, I began to tell some of my story to others who I believed to be trustworthy. They would become my support system and my lifeline when, once again, I would face another one of the most difficult memories that would surface.

Chapter 15

After Three Decades…
Allowance

The moment I realized I was pissed off to be alive was a shocking one! About a month prior to this epiphany, I had begun remembering the details of what I, up to this point, believe was the last time the abuse had taken place. One of the most frustrating things about the resurfacing of repressed memories is the inability to recall every detail at any given time. Many times, only a brief remembrance is provided. Usually there are many specifics that are left unknown. This is where your conscious mind begins not only to try to fill in the missing links but also to understand the incidentals.

The surfacing of the memory of the last abuse attempt set me back many steps in my healing journey. I had come so far and made such progress and yet, I so easily fell back into my mode of devastation I had not allowed myself to experience for so long. I was paralyzed. Suddenly, as though with one fell-swoop, I found myself at the bottom of the depths within and unable to see my way back to some form of well being or reality. It seemed the more I was able to uncover about this particular memory, the more I was literally giving up in my life at the present time. The memory unfolded in this way...

I was fourteen years old and was strong enough to physically fight back. At this age, I now had an understanding that the abuse was wrong and I came to understand what the names he'd called me throughout the years actually meant. I was sick. Sick to my stomach, sick of the verbal, physical, and sexual abuse. Even the fact that he would beat me into submission each time by hitting my ears and head where the bruises wouldn't show was not enough to keep me from fighting with all I had this time.

An encounter with one of the perpetrator's sons (who I had initially believed had been so instrumental in my sense of relief the night of the dreaded "Christmas kiss request") was what gave me the courage to move forward in the planning and strategizing of an event so unthinkable and unimaginable. When he, too, decided it was his time to take a turn with me, I was much older, much stronger, much more determined and, therefore, successful in warding him off. Though I was unable to escape without physical, mental, and emotional injury, I had protected myself sexually. A huge victory! A victory that would spur me onto the next step in what I believed would be the final stage of my life.

I was now ready for the perpetrator. I knew his routine and I'd been planning my strategy for months. I would fight with all I had since my plan was to kill him, literally, and then kill myself. I was in eighth grade and had lost the will to live. Life had become too overwhelming for me. I couldn't, nor did I want to try to survive another day. With him dead, I could be sure that my family members would finally be safe and I would no longer be needed to protect them.

As he began to approach me, I knew his intentions all too well from previous experiences. When the situation presented itself, I became very stoic. With such certainty and conviction, I stated with sincerity that I was going to kill him. At that very moment, there was absolutely no fear running through my body (as there usually was) but instead, sheer determination.

Recognizing the seriousness of my intention and the fact that I was old enough and physically strong enough to actually be able to do as I was professing, he lunged toward me saying, "Not if I kill you first!" Because of his lack of hesitation, I was taken off guard and he was able to get the head start toward my throat he needed to be successful. Cutting off my airway completely, I quickly lost consciousness. As I began to drift through various stages of unconsciousness, I struggled less and felt more at peace. I allowed myself to let go and just drift. For the first time in a very, very long time, I felt completely safe. It was at this moment I made the decision that I wasn't going back. That is, I would not be returning to my body. At 14 years old, my life on this earth plane was over and I was fine with that.

Sometime during this process, a sense of responsibility for my family washed over me and I knew I had to go back. When I returned to my world and regained consciousness, everything, and yet nothing had changed. I felt the all too familiar burden of my heavy body and mind. The sense of security and safety I'd been lavished with only moments before was gone completely. And once again, I was alone, afraid, and truly unwell on many levels. The secret life would resume. Life, as I knew it, went on with a constant need to look over my shoulder and a continued repression of memories.

Though my plan didn't go as I had intended, he, on some level, saved my life. In the end, I had accomplished my goal, since to this day, I believe the abuse never took place again!

Despite the recollection of the "victorious" memory, I was quickly spiraling downward to a place I recognized all too well. In the past, I spoke of my son as being my purpose for remaining on this earth. I love that child more than anything! So when I began to reason that he and his dad had a great relationship and he'd be fine without me, I recognized immediately that I was going even deeper into the depths than I'd ever gone.

It was at this time that I was fortunate enough to have worked during the previous years on setting up a support system for myself comprised of friends and professionals. Luckily, they noticed; they cared enough; they reached out to me; they picked me up, took my hand, led me to where they knew I needed to be, and literally saved me. I had left my body, or dissociated, once again to such a degree that I'd had only little awareness of the state I was in. It wasn't until they'd led me to the avenues of help that had, up to this point, been so successful in my healing that I became aware of where I had unknowingly allowed myself to go.

Over the years of healing work, the many "tools" I'd devised and added to my "survival tool kit" were key in providing a stable framework to catch me whenever a new layer of repression (such as this one) would unfold. When dealing with the initial layers, I would revert back, as though by default, to isolation. This was the original survival technique I learned very quickly as a young child when I experienced the initial acts of abuse.

However, the unfolding of each successive layer of abuse provided me with the opportunity to devise and put into practice the newly attained theory of reaching out for support from those I'd felt certain could do so without any detriment caused to them. This supportive framework consisted of friends, trained professionals in the area of abuse, body workers, some family members, etc. They agreed to be aware of my actions or lack thereof (which pointed to my reverting back to isolation), to check in occasionally when they noticed I wasn't reaching out, and to be aware of my behaviors that would mimic those I'd devised at a young age. Yes, those strategies had helped me to survive back then but now I had other tools that helped me not only to just get through such times but also to flourish despite them.

All my life, I'd taken a vow of secrecy. It had become ingrained in me to remain silent about anything surrounding the abuse. At times, that meant fabricating stories necessary for covering up any emotional displays that caught the attention of others. Though natural and healthy for the body to release overwhelming emotions being held within, it was too dangerous for me to do so. On rare occasions when the truth threatened to unfold, I directed the attention as far from the truth as possible. "I'm just tired," I'd lie, or "I'm not really feeling well." Often, I'd even use, "Financially, I'm overwhelmed!" Anything that was believable that wasn't the truth!

As time went on, I would begin to break that vow of secrecy one step at a time disclosing carefully chosen information to only those I was certain would keep my secret.

Still further along the timeline of my healing journey, I learned how to ask for what I needed. When those circumstances arose that did not allow for the opportunity to divert attention nor to carefully think through and plan a strategy for dealing with the truth, I needed to just ask for what I knew would help in that moment of crisis. The experiencing of body remembrances were such times.

One occasion was on my way back from a Christmas shopping weekend with my sisters. Though I'd planned ahead and taken my own vehicle to allow for my departure without imposing upon anyone else, I was unable to shield them from what took place on our way home. I'd been experiencing discomfort in my neck and pain in my right shoulder (the spot that held a great deal of emotion) for several hours. I recognized these signs all too well and knew it could be the manifestation of a body remembrance.

When such an episode took place, it felt as though I was physically and emotionally experiencing the abuse at that very moment. Such an event had the potential to last anywhere from several minutes to a number of hours. A few of them had sent me to the emergency room; initially when I experienced my first body remembrance and had no idea what was happening and then another time when my body was unable to bring an end to the episode on its own.

This particular time, I felt the panic wash over me as I followed my sisters on the drive towards home. Luckily, we were on a highway and near a rest stop. I went into autopilot and called my sisters to tell them I was "freaking out". Somehow we crossed three lanes of traffic and made it safely into the rest stop area. By this time, the physical aspects of the body remembrance began to manifest. It felt as though I was experiencing the abuse at that very moment. Though my mind knew differently, my body still perceived imminent danger.

I had been through enough of these episodes to know that I needed to have a sense of security. I laid down on the bench in the rest area building and asked one sister to hold onto my legs and the other just held my upper body. This would allow me a sense of protection and support. After some time, though unable to drive myself the rest of the way home, I was able to allow my sisters to get me home safely.

What they experienced that night was beyond my ability from which I could shelter them. Though I was able to ask for what I needed, I wasn't able to give them a whole lot of other details since my mind and body were focused on my perceived lack of safety at that moment. When they'd taken it upon themselves to contact my husband who'd seen me experience a few of these body remembrances, he reassured them that it would take time for the episode to pass and that they were doing exactly what I needed them to do.

* * * * *

When I began to go through the realization that something so devastating had impacted me, there couldn't help but be a change in my personality on some level. The false sense of security I'd created through illusions in my life dropped away and I had to learn to temporarily live a life (though at the time, I didn't realize it would be temporary) seemingly stripped of any sense of familiarity. My view of what constituted truth and its definitive impact no longer held true for me. So, of course, it brought about the need to redefine my life on so many levels. Throughout that process, my personality (as well as my actions) was altered from that which everyone found familiar in me. Often, others who knew what I was going through didn't know what to say or how to act. The parameters of relationships seemed to shift and there was a period of adjustment for all involved.

Often, well-intentioned people didn't realize it wasn't necessary for them to fix me or my circumstances nor did they realize they could be supportive by just listening. Some, particularly those who'd been through life-altering experiences, were able to empathetically display appropriate supportive actions and words. These individuals recognized the stages of healing and did not fear my displays of emotions. They were able to see when I was stuck and unable to move forward into the next stage of healing. However, they were also the individuals who knew to lovingly, and at times assertively, encourage me to move forward through the use of imagination and strategy. They'd help me to imagine what it would be like to take the next healing step. Then if I were comfortable with that, they'd help me to devise a strategy or plan to do so.

It was very important for me to know (especially during times of crisis) that I ultimately had the final say in choosing and implementing options. Individuals impacted by abuse of any kind often are not given choices. They are not allowed to play a role in the outcome of those choices nor given the opportunity to understand the healthy relationship between cause and effect. They learn what happens only at that moment when events are forcibly unfolding. There is no dialogue or compromising. The only avenues they understand are one-way streets that are always in direct opposition to "their" way.

Being forced into making a decision about a situation they are not comfortable with (however well-intentioned the helpful individuals may be) could only cause them to feel as though they are being backed into a "proverbial" corner. This could very likely mimic past events and trigger unhealthy old, outdated coping strategies. There's a good possibility these individuals had been backed into literal physical corners many times in their lives with the knowledge of only two options; to fight or flee. More often than not, it's likely neither of these choices yielded positive results for them in the past.

Though I had worked diligently at attaining all these "tools" in my repertoire, my work was not done yet. Life continued to be a struggle and the only piece left untouched that seemed to be of great importance in reaching the next level of healing was that of my family. I was still keeping my secret from my family members. Yes, my sisters knew very few pieces of my past, but only the ones I'd allowed myself to share with them. My parents knew even less. I had told them very little and even when I was falling apart throughout the previous years, I'd always made excuses or given other reasons for my turmoil or my deficient health. I was still keeping that secret within myself. Even when I told the few people I'd allowed in, I was always fearful that somehow, my family would accidentally hear of it, and I would have failed in keeping their emotional well-being in tact.

Allowing the possibility of telling my family my story had been a topic of conversation many times during my counseling sessions. I was always adamant that the detriment of disclosing to them would far outweigh the healing benefits for me. It was my belief (as is the case with most abusive situations) that the effects and consequences of my actions needed to be weighed very carefully since there were many people, aside from myself, who could be impacted and greatly affected on many levels. However, during one particular session, my counselor said something to me that would, for some reason, make me stop and take notice as well as actually encourage me to change my way of thinking even if only on a small scale.

She said, "You are only as sick as your secrets!" She went on to say how I'd been so busy trying to hide my secret in order to protect everyone that I wasn't allowing myself to take care of me. She even encouraged me to look at it as though it may be a component of healing for my family. Because of their love for me, they had all been affected by witnessing the pain I'd experienced, the confusion of not understanding the root of that pain, and the frustration of not knowing how to help. I was sickened to think that my well-intended actions to protect my family could actually be causing more "trauma". Viewing such a disclosure as an opportunity to help heal my family was a very different and positive perspective from the one I'd held onto for so many years.

As I began to reassess my mode of healing, my counselor allowed me a sense of control in that ultimately, it was my decision. We discussed what some disclosure options would be and kept in mind that it would be a "process and not an event". There would be no time limit for the development and completion of a disclosure plan. She even offered to be present during my disclosure if I so chose.

Over the next few sessions, we looked at the number of friends and professionals I'd allowed to support me in my healing journey. It gave me such a sense of pleasure to see how I'd actually allowed myself to trust others and let them support me from time to time. Then we made a list of family members that I would possibly be able to tell. For each of those on that list, we brainstormed the type of support I would want to have in place for them to ensure that their sense of well-being would remain in tact.

It took me quite some time to decide which family member I would tell and whether I would actually tell at all. When I finally gained the courage to tell someone, I chose my sister. I called and spoke with her and asked if she'd be willing to come in for a counseling session with me.

When the day finally arrived, my counselor was of great comfort, support, and guidance to both my sister and me. I told many of the details about the repressed memories that had made their way to the surface over the last six or seven years. It was one of the most difficult things I had to do as an adult. Even at that point, I had not been able to convince myself that my disclosure was in the best interest of all concerned. However, I was learning to trust not only myself but also others. This was a huge lesson in faith.

Although there were tears, my sister admitted that what I had disclosed was very similar to what she had only imagined over the years. That day was about confirmation. I was shocked and relieved. My sister and I went back to her house and talked for several more hours. By the time I left, I felt a sense of satisfaction not only that the disclosure was over, but also that she was not mentally and emotionally maimed. I felt a great deal lighter. Just knowing my "secret" had been openly and honestly revealed to and just as importantly, believed by, someone I held so dear was healing in itself.

She was able to help me with major decisions about what to do in regards to my other family members. Should I disclose to my other sister? Did my parents need to know? Would it cause more harm than good? It felt so freeing to have someone else who had just as much insight into my family's dynamics and who could assist me in making educated, quality decisions as to which avenues would be the most beneficial and the least detrimental. For the first time, I had allowed a family member to support me. The release of pressure was incredible.

Throughout the ensuing weeks, my sister and I would connect on a very regular basis just to check in. Her comments to me were more healing than she could have ever imagined. She was my new source of validation. Things that I'd chastised myself for being so sensitive about or for having such difficulties with were put into perspective by just hearing the words she spoke to me. I was now able to see myself as a person of strength versus one with many weaknesses. This, too, was very healing and helped me to see myself in a more positive light.

When she agreed to be a support to me, she took on a possible responsibility of having the pressure of being my "spokesperson". She now had my permission to give out information to any family members who could have potentially asked. My only advice to her before disseminating this information was to ask them if they truly wanted to know and if so, then she could tell them all she knew. In this way, she was my buffer and my partner in some of the decision-making. Once again, I'd allowed her to become a source of support as she had been so many times in the past.

Chapter 16

Repercussions of Abuse on
Spirituality and Sense of Self

I n this chapter, I risk repeating much of the story already told
and yet, if you are using this as a handbook and seeking out only
those chapters relevant to your particular need at a particular
time, cross-referencing may be necessary. Therefore, I have included
references to previous chapters that could help to illuminate points
being made here.

Having been born and raised with strict religious practices, I
knew at an early age the avenues to avoid so as not to burn eternally
in hell. However, though try as I might to avoid it, it appeared that
that was exactly where I was headed.

As I progressed in years, things that hadn't ever entered my mind
about the repercussions of the abuse began to become crystal clear to
me. It was very frightening on a whole new "spiritual" level! Though
taught never to lie, where even white lies were questionable, I was
doing so on such a deep scale in order to assure that the truth about
the abuse would never be revealed! The biggest sin I was committing
was unwillingly partaking in premarital sex, an absolute No-No not
only in the church's eyes but in the rules of my family. I was a sinner
and yet repentance wasn't even an option for me.

When I was in high school, the perpetrator died. Though he no longer posed a threat to my family or me, the damage had been done. Now being a teenager and dating, I had to make more decisions related to sex. It just became overwhelming. Though on a different level with different circumstances, it seemed as though I was still battling sin on a daily basis and the joys were not enough to offset all the pain experienced in my life.

As an adult, I was so very repressed on all levels of being. More often than not, I was miserable and just unhappy with almost everything (except my son) in my life. I couldn't have found joy if it knocked me down and dragged me around. There was such an irony to it. I would hear my thoughts, listen to my spoken words, feel the emotions that felt all too real to me and yet, when I'd examine my life and all that I had, I felt like such an ungrateful human being.

As a teacher, I was all too aware that abuse tends to repeat in a generational pattern. I was sick when this knowledge bumped up with the realization that I could, as the research indicated, become a perpetrator. Here I had access to so many young lives and the possibility that I could potentially do such a thing was sickening to me. Reassurance from my counselor about the positive impact an "abuse victim's" awareness as well as their family upbringing can have only validated what I knew in my heart and soul I would never do and, in fact, would fight to my last breath to prevent. Aside from the wonderful love I experienced through my son, the rest of my life felt too oppressive and I wanted nothing to do with it.

However, my religious beliefs spoke of a Being who sacrificed his very son as well as a man who sacrificed his own life for my redemption. Yet, I wanted no part of that life that had been so selflessly saved. "How ungrateful!" I would reprimand myself. Chastising myself, I would bring on more self-hate that left me feeling beaten, battered, and defeated.

Years later, I would recall yet another sin I so closely came to committing. Only this time, it would be a sin that I would choose to commit through my own free will. Though the perpetrator was not physically in my presence on a daily basis, his threats of never knowing when he'd be there (Chapter 11) had me in constant fear and always watchful. I never got any relief!

Despite my knowledge of the church's teaching that suicide would definitely buy me a ticket to damnation of my soul, it no longer mattered to me. I figured I was heading there anyway and at least this would allow the hell on earth to finally cease. So, as explained in Chapter 9, I began plotting my own death. I realized it would have to be well thought out so as not to leave anything undone. Doing so would put too many of my loved ones in danger. Because I viewed myself as my family's only guardian, I was the buffer between him and them. If I were gone, what would happen to their safety and well being?

Upon acknowledgement of what I knew as "truth", it was decided. I realized there was no other option but to eliminate the perpetrator (Chapter 11) before I could take my own life. I would actually attempt to take the life of another human being. Now I was planning a murder.

Not only was that against the laws of the land, but it was also a mortal sin to take the life of another! However, at age 14 and living amidst the constant fear of his threats, I saw no other option. Throughout this whole planning process, the incident with the perpetrator's son's abuse attempt (Chapter 11) validated my sense of knowing that I could, and would, be strong enough mentally and physically to pull off what needed to be done! Luckily, I was unsuccessful on both counts and the perpetrator saved me from committing two very mortal sins in the eyes of my faith.

However, decades later, as an adult, the realization of my serious attempt to take the life of another living, breathing, human being hit me with such devastation. I began to look at myself as having similar qualities to those in public institutions and jails who'd successfully completed a plan similar to my own as an adolescent child.

Though I viewed myself as a good person who had compassion and empathy (sometimes to my own detriment) for other living beings, I was in disbelief at this remembrance of my intentions. I was the one who swerved to avoid hitting even the smallest of creatures. I was the one who had to pull over to the side of the road to regain my composure the day I was unsuccessful at avoiding one such creature. And yet, I had such heinous intentions for another human being?

Years before, I had left the only church I'd known and was sort of floundering. Though I still had a strong belief in the Divine, I felt very alone and unsure if I was rationalizing my decision to do so in order to make myself feel better about whom I was as a person. Luckily, at the time of the recollection of the murder/suicide memory, I had begun to explore another church. It had many of the same core beliefs as the church of my childhood, yet allowed for the human traits of imperfection, compassion, and tolerance without judgment.

I was struggling to such a degree with this newly acquired memory that I decided to meet with the pastor of this church I'd incorporated into my life. I'd grown to respect this man so deeply merely by listening to him speak the Divine's words on a weekly basis. Despite the fact I didn't often trust others with even simple matters, I knew I needed to confide in him about my most well-kept secret. I'd spoken with him on one previous occasion but revealed nothing of my abusive past.

I showed up without warning at the church on a Wednesday morning. There was something taking place at that time in the auditorium. Seeing him speaking with someone in the hallway, I approached and asked if it would be possible to speak with him. Without hesitation, he walked with me to an area where there could be some privacy.

I spared no details in telling him of the recollection of my intentions as a teenager. I shared with him my lack of self-forgiveness and revealed my belief that I needed Divine forgiveness on this one. He listened intently as it was obvious I was struggling emotionally to reveal what I perceived to be the shameful, honest truth about myself.

As I fumbled with my words, my mind kept wondering if he was feeling uncomfortable in my presence. Was he fearful of his safety at that moment? After all, he was with this horrible person capable of committing such a terrible crime.

I finished speaking and he began. (As I write this, I am welling up with tears of gratitude). Again, without hesitation or even taking a moment to come to grips with what I believe was shocking information, the pastor spoke with certainty.

He revealed his belief that there, in fact, was no need for Divine forgiveness. He went on to say that even before I'd thought about the plan, I was forgiven. He believed it to be a Divinely inspired plan and that it was the Divine's grace that intervened and allowed that 14-year-old to believe she could actually carry out such a plan. He then encouraged me to shift my thinking about the whole matter.

He shared his thoughts on how my attempt on the perpetrator's life may have been the Divine's plan to stop the abuse not only for me but possibly (and most likely) many others in the perpetrator's path. He assured me that had I been successful in my attempt, it would have been viewed as an act of survival for myself and my family. He went on in stating that he believed that even a court of law would have seen it as a child's attempt to survive.

The pastor continued by saying that instead of writing a letter of forgiveness to that 14- year-old girl (as had been discussed in a previous counseling session), a letter of thanks might be more appropriate. It could include thankfulness for her willingness to accept the Divine's plan to end the abuse as well as her courage to follow through with it.

Other extremely helpful pieces of information were shared throughout that discussion. Yet, I feel with every sense of my being that the most valuable piece of my meeting with this man doing the Divine's important work is the way I walked away from that church that day. Only twenty minutes before, I'd walked in broken and so very certain I did not deserve to be a part of this earth's existence. Leaving, I felt whole. I viewed myself as courageous instead of horrid. I felt for the first time like I finally deserved the breath of life in my lungs; something that I'd deemed myself undeserving of for most of my life. I was changed because I'd received healing words and perspectives from a very nonjudgmental Divine worker. I will be forever grateful beyond the expression of words to that pastor and the kindness he showed me.

Afterword

As enlightening and rewarding as gaining acceptance of my life's circumstances and the healing that it brought forth can be, it was not as easy as one would think. I needed not only to understand who I was as a person, but also the reasons why I lived the way I did within my world. That meant realizing the fact that who I had become was formed by what I had encountered throughout my life. Once I became very clear about who I was and why I was that way, I had to decide who I wanted to be. With this knowledge, I could then weed through those things that were in line with my goals and intentions and release those things that were not. Self-realizations had to become self-actualizations in order to bring about any lasting changes.

That was a difficult process until I realized that it wasn't just about what I viewed to be my deficits but how my experiences had actually brought out my courage, strengths, and capacity to persevere as well as my compassion, empathy, and deep understanding for others.

It allowed me to focus on who I was on the inside versus who I looked to be to others on the outside. However, it came with the necessity to learn to set healthy boundaries in my life that would benefit me while not infringing upon others' rights to be who they needed to be. In doing so, I often had to look beyond the superficial triggers in order to lovingly release those situations and people in my life that were not allowing my own growth and truth. Most importantly, I needed to learn the difference between "self-ishness" and "self-care".

Another large lesson for me was allowing people to really "be" in my life. Not just on a superficial level, but on a level that would require vulnerability on my part if these relationships were going to grow to be of any depth at all. Vulnerability is an issue that can often be intimidating for a multitude of people regardless of their life challenges.

Through the healing process, not only did my inner world change but also my outer world. It was about restructuring my life to fit my authentic self that I had finally allowed to appear. These changes would better complement my life as I chose to experience it. Difficult? Yes. But also rewarding and empowering.

In deciding how to close this story that is not yet complete, I decided to do so in a poem. I now leave you with the following words and my gratitude-filled, heartfelt intention for a showering of love upon you and yours. May love and blessings be with you always!

Who Is This Woman

I remember the days when she was fearful and meek
When despite the situation, no words she would speak
She was always careful to be sure everyone understood
Her actions and behaviors were used to convince she was "good".
Always careful of which emotions she dared to reveal
Her life she orchestrated to hide the surreal
Just why this was necessary, she could not comprehend
Her life was based on the idea "defend, don't offend".
Then that one fateful day it all came together
The world she had built crumbled under a feather
She began to realize why things were as they were
But the light at the end just remained a blur.
Try as she may to rid herself of doubt
It seemed from that tunnel she may never come out
Yet, in the moment of her deepest despair
Encouraging words she did manage to hear.
She began listening to her soul's cries from within
Which gave her the push to try once again
This time she quieted and listened to the inner chatter
And realized she'd neglected HER truth in the matter.
Though not an easy task to do initially
She checked in with herself emotionally and physically
Then with the information she did move forward
To allow the truth despite how horrid.
That's when the true healing finally began
Life unfolded in a way possible only through Divine plan
Though what she'd endured would never be forgotten
She chose to focus on the woman it had begotten.